CORPORATE ★ AMERICA

JPMORGAN CHASE

Tammy Gagne

LIGHTBOX
openlightbox.com

Lightbox is an all-inclusive digital solution for the teaching and learning of curriculum topics in an original, groundbreaking way. Lightbox is based on National Curriculum Standards.

STANDARD FEATURES OF LIGHTBOX

AUDIO High-quality narration using text-to-speech system

ACTIVITIES Printable PDFs that can be emailed and graded

SLIDESHOWS Pictorial overviews of key concepts

VIDEOS Embedded high-definition video clips

WEBLINKS Curated links to external, child-safe resources

TRANSPARENCIES Step-by-step layering of maps, diagrams, charts, and timelines

INTERACTIVE MAPS Interactive maps and aerial satellite imagery

QUIZZES Ten multiple choice questions that are automatically graded and emailed for teacher assessment

KEY WORDS Matching key concepts to their definitions

Contents

Introduction

With a 200-year history, JPMorgan Chase is one of the oldest financial institutions in the United States. The company serves millions of clients in more than 60 countries. These clients range from everyday people to some of the largest corporations in the world.

In addition to being one of the best-known names in the financial industry, JPMorgan Chase is also one of the world's largest banks in terms of value. The company's **assets** total about $2.6 trillion. Its **stock** is part of the Dow Jones Industrial Average. The 30 stocks that make up this list are considered to be among the most influential in the world.

Nearly 1/2 of all U.S. households do business with JPMorgan Chase.

JPMorgan Chase has *more than* 3,000 **financial advisors** on staff.

Approximately 28.4 million people use the company's mobile services.

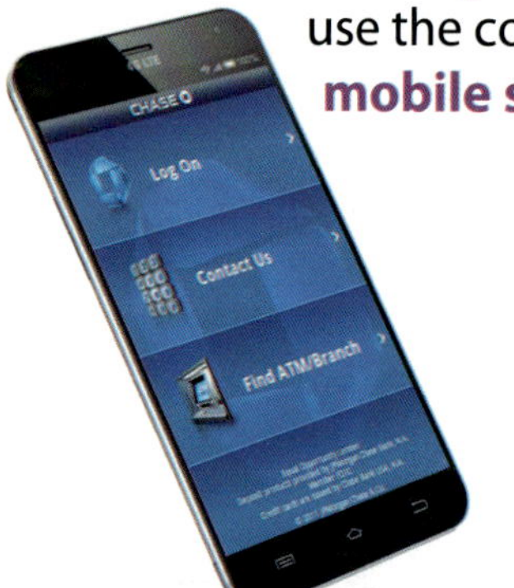

JPMorgan Chase has more than 18,000 ATMs in the United States *alone*.

JPMorgan Chase has more than 5,300 branch offices across the United States. It currently has a presence in 30 of the country's 50 states.

Founding Date	Became Public	Opening Price	Stock Symbol
1799	December 30, 1983	$44.00 USD	nyse: JPM

Beginnings

The history of JPMorgan Chase is long and diverse. The company that exists today is actually the product of about 1,200 different businesses that have come together over the last two centuries. Among them were J.P. Morgan & Co. and Chase Manhattan Bank—the two former businesses for which the company is now named.

In the late 1790s, banks were much different than they are today. Before a company could provide banking services, it needed a **charter** from the state legislature. The process for obtaining this document was long and difficult, so few banking businesses existed. Each bank had a **monopoly** in the area in which it did business. The Manhattan Company, one of the many businesses behind JPMorgan Chase, was one of the first companies to introduce competition into the banking industry.

The Manhattan Company began as a water company when it was founded by a group of businessmen in 1799. One of the key founders was Aaron Burr, who would later become vice president of the United States. Burr created the water company with a special provision in its charter. It enabled The Manhattan Company to use its excess **capital** to provide banking services. By September 1799, The Bank of The Manhattan Company had opened for business. In 1955, it joined with Chase National Bank to form Chase Manhattan Bank.

Besides his interest in railroads, J.P. Morgan also played a key role in establishing United States Steel Corporation, General Electric, and other iconic U.S. corporations.

Almost a century after The Manhattan Company was founded, John Pierpont Morgan established a banking business with partner Anthony Drexel. The son of a successful banker, Morgan had made a name for himself by bailing out struggling railroads in the 19th century. The bank, which eventually became known as J.P. Morgan & Co., continued long after Morgan's death in 1913. In 2000, it **merged** with Chase Manhattan, forming the company as it is known today.

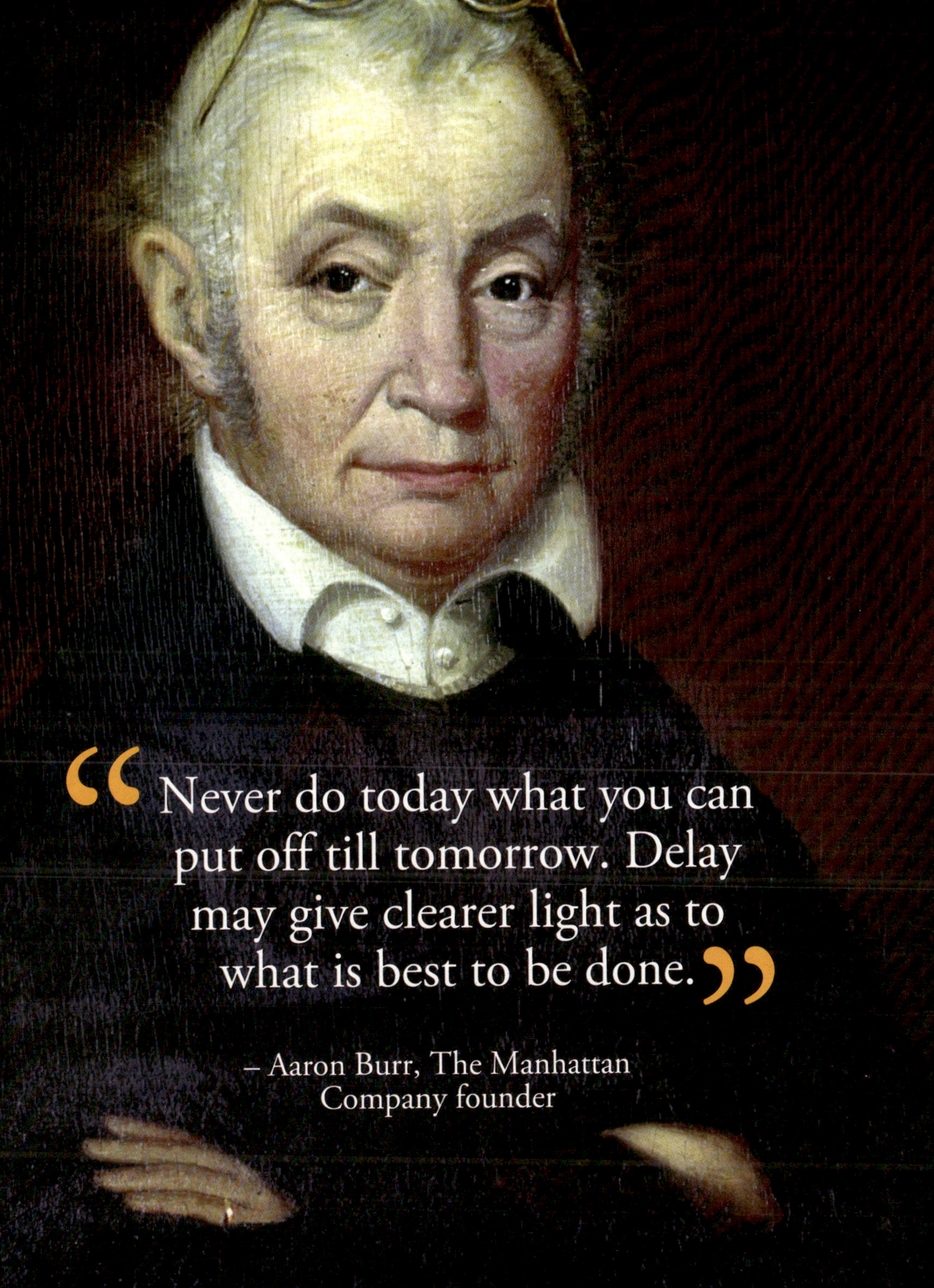
"Never do today what you can put off till tomorrow. Delay may give clearer light as to what is best to be done."
– Aaron Burr, The Manhattan Company founder

Corporate Timeline

JPMorgan Chase's success is the result of many business deals over a long period of time. The list of companies that helped form JPMorgan Chase features two centuries' worth of financial leaders. With each merger or **acquisition**, the company took another step toward becoming the comprehensive financial institution it is today.

A New Venture
John Pierpont Morgan and Anthony Drexel found Drexel, Morgan & Co.

In Business
The Manhattan Company receives its charter.

A Change in Name
Drexel, Morgan & Co. is reorganized as J.P. Morgan & Co. following Drexel's death.

1799

1871

1895

1877

1955

Joining Forces
The Bank of The Manhattan Company and Chase National Bank merge to form Chase Manhattan Bank.

Banking on Success
Chase National Bank is founded by John Thompson. It is named for Salmon P. Chase, who served as the secretary of the treasury under Abraham Lincoln.

Merge and Move JPMorgan Chase merges with Bank One Corporation, a leader in **consumer banking**.

Under New Ownership Chase Manhattan merges with Chemical Banking Corporation. The company retains the name Chase Manhattan.

A Burst of Energy JPMorgan Chase buys The Bear Stearns Companies, Inc., adding energy trading to its long list of services.

1996

2004

2008

2000

2017

Coming Together J.P. Morgan and Chase Manhattan merge to form JPMorgan Chase.

A Private Matter JPMorgan Chase partners with Zcash to develop new privacy features for its digital banking services.

JPMorgan Chase Today

Today, JPMorgan Chase offers a wide selection of banking and **investment** services to its clients. JPMorgan Chase's products can be divided into four basic categories. These are consumer and community banking, corporate and investment banking, **commercial banking**, and asset and wealth management.

JPMorgan Chase's consumer products range from checking and savings accounts to credit cards, car loans, and **mortgages**. Much of the company's consumer business is conducted at the branch level, with clients visiting their local branch to make deposits and withdrawals. Some people may also meet with bank employees to discuss their banking options. Many of the services offered at the consumer level can also be accessed online.

At the corporate level, JPMorgan Chase offers more advanced banking services. One of the more common services is providing large-scale loans to corporations. The bank can also help companies raise capital for ventures such as buying out other businesses. Corporations may also turn to JPMorgan Chase for advice about other financial aspects of their businesses.

One of the bank's best-known branches can be found in New York City's Times Square. The sign above the entrance is one of the largest high-definition displays in the world.

Banking services for commercial clients include **treasury services** and real estate financing. For instance, when a town or city needs to upgrade its roads or bridges, JPMorgan Chase can assist by lending the money for construction. It can also sell **bonds** to raise money for these projects.

JPMorgan Chase's asset and wealth management services help people and businesses invest money to create future wealth. For example, clients can open an individual retirement account (IRA) with JPMorgan Chase to help them save money for their later years. Businesses may have JPMorgan Chase create retirement plans for their employees.

"The best way to look at any business is from the standpoint of the clients."
– James Dimon, JPMorgan Chase **Chief Executive Officer (CEO)**

A World of JPMorgan Chase

JPMorgan Chase remains one of the best-known banks in the United States. Over the years, it has extended its reach into the international market. Today, the company has a strong global presence.

ARCTIC OCEAN

NORTH AMERICA

PACIFIC OCEAN

1

SOUTH AMERICA

2

ATLANTIC OCEAN

MAP LEGEND

Featured Location

Land

Water

0 1,000 Miles

1,000 Kilometers

SOUTHERN OCEAN

ANTARCTICA

1 **Corporate Headquarters** JPMorgan Chase's world headquarters is located on Park Avenue in New York City. This office focuses on investing, wealth planning, and credit and banking.

2 **South America** JPMorgan Chase has been serving clients in Brazil for more than 50 years. The Brazil operations, including those in Rio de Janeiro, specialize in investments, credit, wealth planning, and **philanthropic** planning.

3 **European Headquarters** JPMorgan Chase's main European office is located in London, England. This corporate office offers the same services to its clients as its sister location across the Atlantic Ocean.

4 **Middle East** JPMorgan Chase's office in the United Arab Emirates is located in the affluent city of Dubai. The office offers corporate and investment banking services.

5 **Asia** The company's investment arm, J.P. Morgan, has its Asia-Pacific headquarters in Hong Kong. Besides investments, the office provides wealth management and lending services.

Branding JPMorgan Chase

One of the biggest challenges financial service companies face is building and maintaining a reputation for trustworthiness. This is important because people need to trust the company they turn to for help with their money. As a leader in the industry, JPMorgan Chase has worked hard to **brand** itself as being dependable and honest.

Serving the Client Ensuring its clients feel valued is key to JPMorgan Chase's success. The company focuses on a personalized approach to customer service. It is committed to understanding each client's financial needs and goals. Having this insight allows the company to provide the client with the programs and services that will best help him or her meet these goals. JPMorgan Chase knows that the growth of the company depends on the growth of its clients. It has developed a wide range of products and services designed to meet the needs of all types of clients, whether they are individuals, small businesses, or large companies.

Rooted in Community

It would be easy for a company the size of JPMorgan Chase to serve only certain types of clients. Instead of staying in the area of big business, however, the company has maintained a community focus. In fact, JPMorgan Chase believes that it can use its size to make a difference in the communities it serves. Instead of being an intimidating "big bank," the company promotes itself as having the resources necessary to help everyone.

High Standards JPMorgan Chase wants people to know they can trust the company with their money. To do this, the company's brand emphasizes its commitment to excellence in all that it does. Company employees are expected to conduct themselves with integrity in all client interactions, and to behave ethically at all times. The company's operations are held to the same standards. While JPMorgan Chase understands that missteps will occur, it focuses on learning from these mistakes and improving its systems to avoid a reoccurrence.

JPMorganChase 

Company Name

The merger of The Manhattan Company and Chase National Bank gave JPMorgan Chase half of its modern name. The other half of the company's name came in 2000 when Chase Manhattan merged with J.P. Morgan & Co.

Company Logo

JPMorgan Chase's octagon **logo** has been in use since 1960, although it has changed a bit over the years. While an octagon has no clear connection to banking, as a logo, it provides a quick way for people to recognize the company.

Company Slogan

Companies use advertising **slogans** to help build positive reputations. JPMorgan Chase's goal of building client trust is reflected in the company's current slogan, "The right relationship is everything."

The Art of Selling

Advertising is essential to the success of big companies such as JPMorgan Chase. Even the best financial institutions cannot sell their services if potential clients do not know the company exists. To make sure that people know about JPMorgan Chase and the services it offers, the company has launched multiple advertising campaigns in recent years.

Mastery In 2015, JPMorgan Chase premiered an advertising campaign that featured a variety of well-known people. They included the Rockettes dance company and animal trainer Joel Silverman. The ads paid tribute to the many years of hard work it took for these people to become masters in their respective fields. The commercials ended with all of them mastering the Chase mobile **app** in no time at all, showing the public how user-friendly the company's banking technology is.

Daddy's Little Girl
In 2016, JPMorgan Chase debuted a television commercial showing a father dressing up in a fairy costume for his daughter's birthday party. The commercial offered a touching example of the things parents will do for their children. It later showed the same man dressed in his everyday clothes meeting with a JPMorgan Chase financial advisor to discuss saving for his daughter's education. The ad used humor to promote the importance of saving for college and how JPMorgan Chase can help.

Battle of the Paddle In 2017, JPMorgan Chase featured tennis champion Serena Williams and basketball star Stephen Curry in a television commercial. The two athletes are playing an intense game of ping pong while they wait together to appear on a television show. As the game becomes more competitive, the athletes accidentally break several items in the room. They pay for these accidents using QuickPay, a technology that allows JPMorgan Chase clients to send and receive money in real time. Just seconds after Curry sends $120 for a broken lamp, a message confirming the payment appears on a phone belonging to one of the television crew. The meaning is clear—QuickPay is convenient, fast, and secure.

JPMorgan Chase focuses much of its advertising on customers who are **18 to 35 years old.**

Of all JPMorgan Chase's **new checking account clients, 57% are millennials,** people born between 1982 and 2004.

For every $100 million JPMorgan Chase spends on **advertising,** it gains about **300,000 new households** as clients.

Competitors

Banking is one of the most competitive industries in the world. In order to gain new clients, banks must work hard to convince people that they should do business with them. Some banks focus on leading the way in deposits. Others put their efforts into investments or mortgages. While each bank may have its area of expertise, no business is the top performer in every area of financial services.

WELLS FARGO

STOCK SYMBOL nyse: WFC

Wells Fargo is one of the oldest banks in the United States. With its headquarters in San Francisco, the company has more than 6,000 branches in 39 U.S. states. Wells Fargo offers a variety of services to its clients. These range from standard banking and credit card services to loans for individuals, small businesses, and large corporations.

Bank of America 

STOCK SYMBOL nyse: BAC

Bank of America became the largest wealth management company in the world when it acquired Merrill Lynch in 2008. In 2017, *Forbes* magazine ranked Bank of America as the seventh-largest corporation in the world. Of the top four U.S. banks, it is the only one with operations in all 50 states. Bank of America also does business in more than 35 other countries.

STOCK SYMBOL nyse: C

Citigroup rounds out the top four banks in the United States. Like JPMorgan Chase, Citigroup's headquarters are located in New York. Citigroup stands out among the other banks for doing business with the most foreign nations—more than 160 in all. The company is known for its investment services. It also provides traditional banking services, and has more than 200 million customer accounts.

Comparison Chart

Businesses keep records to track their assets, **liabilities**, **profits**, and losses. Companies use this data to guide expansion and cost-cutting decisions. Investors use the information to help them decide where to invest their money. They will also refer to a company's **market capitalization** to gauge public confidence in the business.

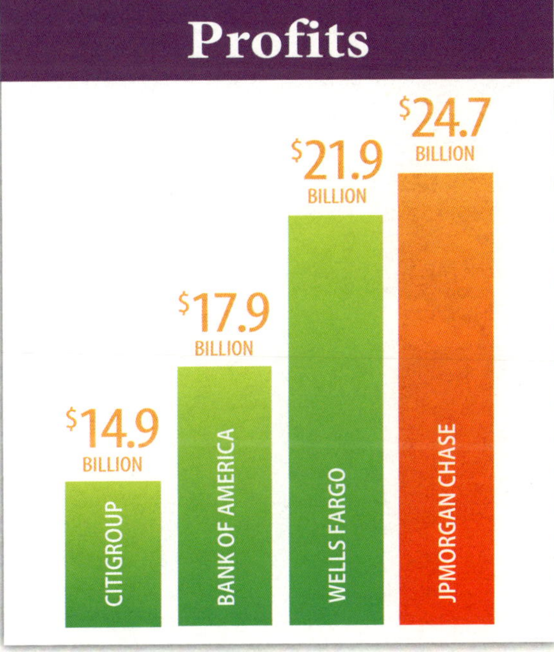

2016 Figures

Innovation and Technology

Zelle

Banks have had the technology to allow clients to pay their bills online for many years. Now, JPMorgan Chase has made it easier for them to move money around in other ways. With the help of a partnership with Zelle Network, JPMorgan Chase clients can use the QuickPay feature in the bank's mobile app to send money to people. The money often appears in the receiver's account in minutes, and the sender never has to leave the security of the JPMorgan Chase app to perform the **transaction**.

TrueCar

Through its partnership with TrueCar, JPMorgan Chase has made the task of finding and financing an automobile much easier. TrueCar, an automotive and pricing information website, works with various auto dealerships throughout the United States. Chase clients can now access TrueCar through the bank's website. Once a client finds the right vehicle, he or she can then apply for a loan and make the purchase on the site.

Roostify

Applying for a mortgage can be a long, painstaking process. Besides all the paperwork a person needs to gather, he or she also has to set up meetings with a mortgage broker to sign forms and review details. To make the process easier for its clients, JPMorgan Chase has partnered with Roostify, an online mortgage application platform. Roostify allows potential home buyers to track their application from beginning to end on their mobile devices.

OnDeck Capital

JPMorgan Chase is bringing small business loans into the new millennium with the help of OnDeck Capital. OnDeck, a non-bank lender, is known for the speed of its technology platform. Applicants receive a faster response on loan requests from OnDeck than they do from traditional banks. JPMorgan Chase is now using this technology to process its own small business loans. The partnership between the two lenders has made it possible for many small businesses to receive same-day or next-day loans from JPMorgan Chase.

Giving Back

Donating time, money, and resources to people in need is one of the most important things a company can do to build a positive image. Many people prefer doing business with companies that give back to the communities they serve. In 2016, JPMorgan Chase donated almost $250 million to **non-profit organizations** around the world.

Workforce Readiness

JPMorgan Chase knows that technology is driving the modern economy. In order to find and keep jobs, people need the skills and knowledge to operate the latest equipment. The company is helping people learn those skills through its New Skills at Work program. This initiative will see JPMorgan Chase provide $250 million over five years to training programs worldwide. A similar program for youth, New Skills for Youth, has also been launched.

Small Business Forward

JPMorgan Chase realizes that small businesses play an important role in growing the economy. The bank's Small Business Forward program focuses on small businesses that are often underserved, such as those owned by women or minorities. Under this program, much of the funding provided by the bank is being given to non-profit organizations that are working to help these underserved businesses. It is meant to connect the businesses with the capital and support networks they need to grow and prosper.

Daily Finance Education No matter how much or how little money a person has, knowing how to manage it properly is essential to one's financial well-being. JPMorgan Chase helps people around the world acquire the skills and tools needed to create sound financial plans. In some cases, this means teaching people how to budget for unexpected expenses. In other situations, it involves showing people how to save for long-term goals. JPMorgan Chase's **pro bono** work in this area ranges from one-on-one financial coaching to large **mentoring** events.

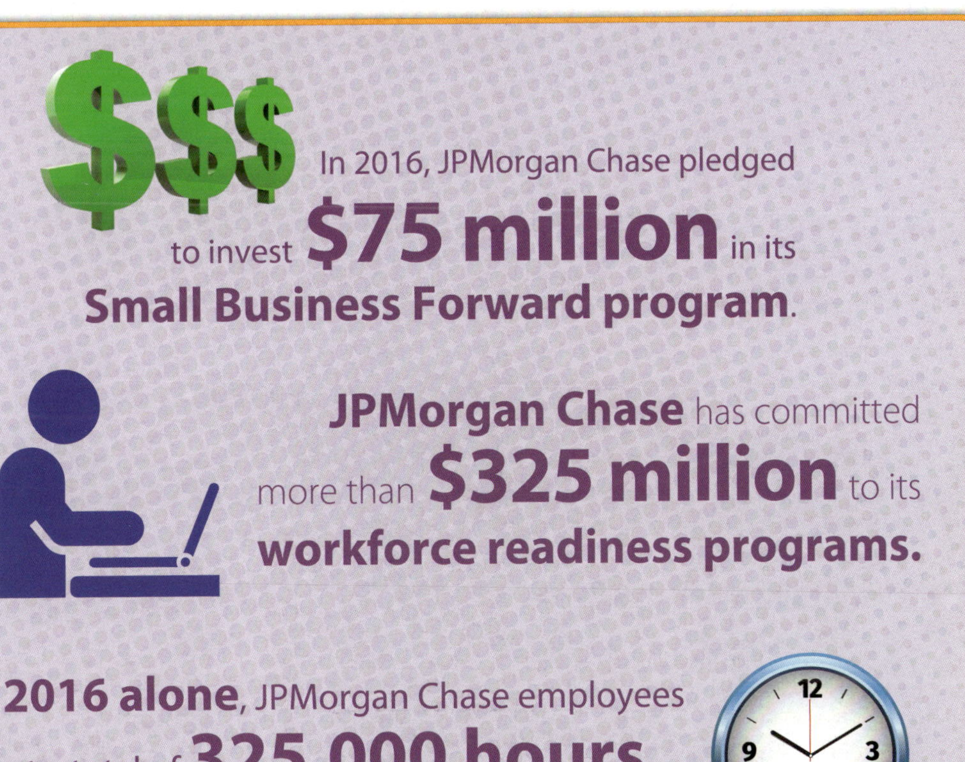

Into the Future

Banking will likely continue to be a highly competitive industry in the future. When it comes to managing their finances, people want the convenience of the latest technology. They also want the potential to grow their money as much as possible. JPMorgan Chase continues to find new ways to meet these needs.

In 2007, JPMorgan Chase introduced Chase Private Client. This program caters to wealthy clients looking to make large-scale investments. The company currently has more than 2,500 Chase Private Client offices. These offices manage investments and deposits totaling $190 billion. The company plans to grow this part of their business even more in the future.

JPMorgan Chase also plans to focus more on the small business sector in the coming years. The company sees a big opportunity in this market. Currently, no single bank has established itself as the primary financial resource for the 28.8 million small businesses that currently operate in the United States. JPMorgan Chase hopes to implement programs and incentives to earn and keep their business as the small companies grow into larger ones.

Keeping an eye on potential competitors is also part of JPMorgan Chase's future plans. The company is paying specific attention to sizable banks from other nations, with Chinese banks being of most concern. As JPMorgan Chase has noted, the top two banks in China are presently almost twice its size in terms of profitability. If JPMorgan Chase is going to hold its own against these competitors, it must start preparing now.

To qualify as a Chase Private Client, customers must have at least $250,000 in deposits or investments.

JPMorgan Chase continues to expand its market through innovative promotions and programs. In 2017, the company partnered with United Airlines to introduce a new credit card. The United TravelBank card will provide users with both cash and travel rewards.

Careers at JPMorgan Chase

The banking industry offers a variety of career paths. JPMorgan Chase employees range from tellers, who work directly with clients, to financial analysts, who study trends in the industry. Each job is important to the success of the company.

Bank Teller

$21,000–$35,000 per year

Bank tellers are often described as the face of the bank. When clients enter a branch, tellers are typically the first employees they see. A teller's basic responsibilities include processing deposits and withdrawals. He or she also handles loan payments and makes foreign currency exchanges. In addition to having good math skills, a bank teller should have a talent for dealing with the public. A friendly, efficient teller helps create a positive impression of the bank to its clients.

Loan Officer

$33,000–$54,000 per year

The primary job of a loan officer is to assist people who are at the bank to apply for a loan. Some clients may be seeking a loan to purchase an automobile or home. Others may be looking for a personal or business loan. In all cases, the loan officer helps guide the client through the application process. Other parts of this job include verifying information supplied by the applicant, such as income level, and making the final decision to approve or deny the loan.

Financial Analyst

$45,000–$118,000 per year

To make money for both its clients and itself, a bank must invest a portion of its assets. It is a financial analyst's job to help banks determine the best ways to accomplish this task. Financial analysts study the industry, searching for trends that show which types of investments will produce the best results. Some financial analysts specialize in one type of investment, such as stocks or bonds.

Senior Executive

$156,000+ per year

Senior executives, such as **chief financial officers** and chief executive officers, are responsible for making key decisions for the company. They establish goals for departments within the bank and the overall company. Senior executives are also in charge of mid-level management positions. Their high level of responsibility requires them to have extensive experience in the banking industry.

Activity

Advertising campaigns are important marketing tools for banks. A successful ad campaign grabs the attention of potential clients. It also lets clients know what the company does, what the company stands for, and how the company can help them personally.

Imagine that you are in charge of an advertising campaign for JPMorgan Chase. Write a plan for a campaign that would showcase the company and its strengths. Consider the following questions when developing your concept.

1. To whom will you target your campaign?
2. Will you place your ads on television, the radio, or the internet?
3. Will you focus on the bank's history, its current programs, or its plans for the future?
4. What will the theme of your campaign be?
5. What other types of promotional materials will you need to create to support your campaign?

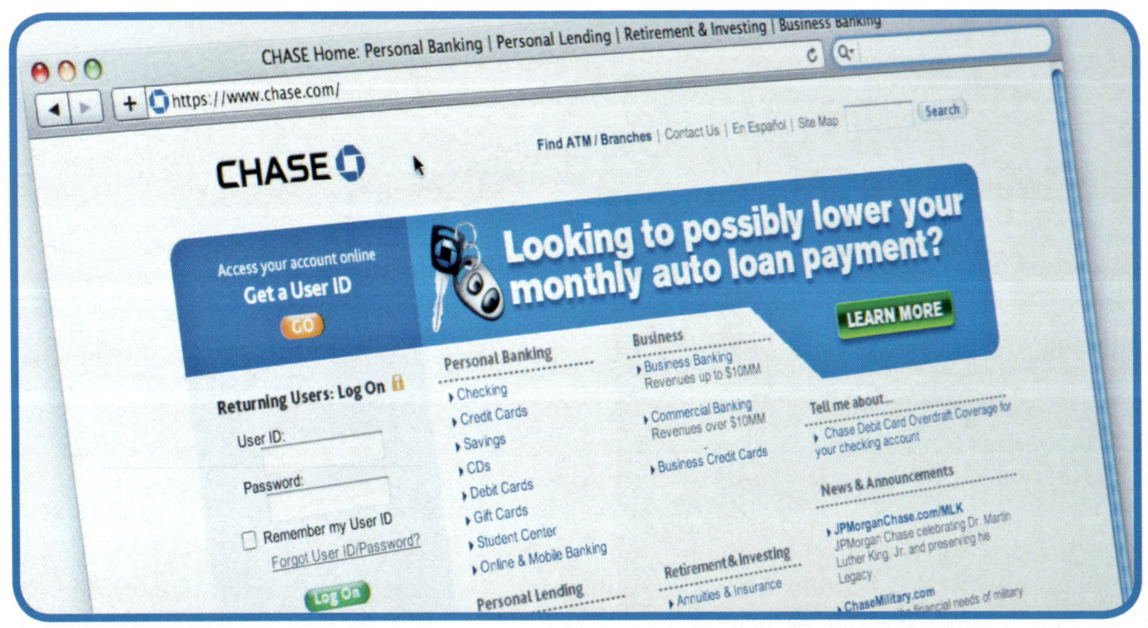

Quiz

1 Where is JPMorgan Chase's headquarters located?

2 Which founder of The Manhattan Company became vice president of the United States?

3 Who founded Chase National Bank?

4 Into which four categories can JPMorgan Chase's products be divided?

5 What is the investment banking arm of JPMorgan Chase called?

6 When did JPMorgan Chase begin using its octagon logo?

7 What is JPMorgan Chase's current slogan?

8 Which of JPMorgan Chase's biggest competitors has branches in all 50 U.S. states?

9 Which non-bank lender has JPMorgan Chase partnered with to provide more small business loans for new companies?

10 Which JPMorgan Chase program helps teach people how to use the latest technology in the workplace?

Answers
1. New York City **2.** Aaron Burr **3.** John Thompson **4.** Consumer and community banking, corporate and investment banking, commercial banking, and asset and wealth management **5.** J.P. Morgan **6.** 1960 **7.** "The right relationship is everything" **8.** Bank of America **9.** OnDeck Capital **10.** New Skills at Work

Key Words

acquisition: the purchase of another company

app: short for application, a software program used on desktop computers and mobile devices

assets: valuable properties owned by a company or person

bonds: signed promises to make a payment on a certain date

brand: to market a company's identity and image

capital: money available for starting a business or investing

charter: a document describing the rights and privileges of an organization

chief executive officer (CEO): the highest-ranking person employed by a company

chief financial officers: the highest-ranking people in charge of finances at a company

commercial banking: banking that focuses on taking deposits and making loans

consumer banking: banking services provided to individuals rather than companies

investment: the commitment of money to a project

liabilities: a company's debts and business costs

logo: a symbol or design used to identify a specific company

market capitalization: the market value of a company's outstanding shares

mentoring: training or advising

merged: came together to form one company

monopoly: the complete control of a service or commodity in an area

mortgages: loans used to buy homes

non-profit organizations: groups that conduct business without a profit motive

philanthropic: making life better for other people

pro bono: work done at no cost to the recipient

profits: the money left over after expenses have been met

slogans: distinctive phrases used to identify a specific company or product

stock: share of a company

transaction: the action of conducting business

treasury services: the management of a company's holdings

Index

LIGHTBOX

SUPPLEMENTARY RESOURCES

Click on the plus icon found in the bottom left corner of each spread to open additional teacher resources.

- Download and print the book's quizzes and activities
- Access curriculum correlations
- Explore additional web applications that enhance the Lightbox experience

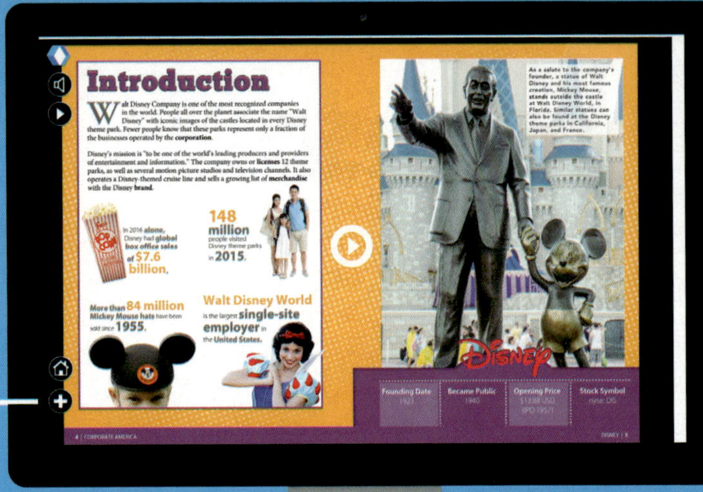

LIGHTBOX DIGITAL TITLES

Packed full of integrated media

VIDEOS

INTERACTIVE MAPS

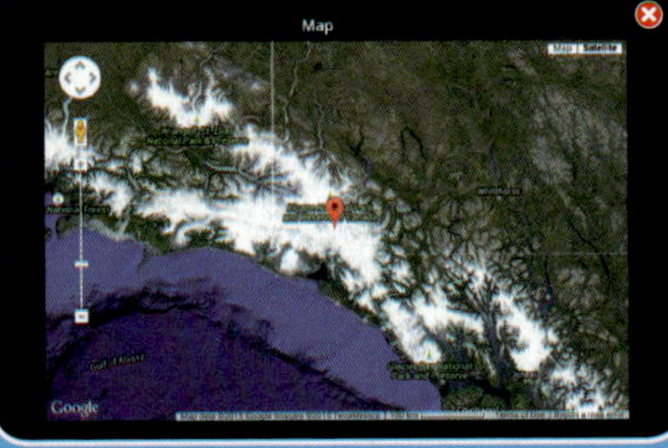

WEBLINKS

SLIDESHOWS

QUIZZES

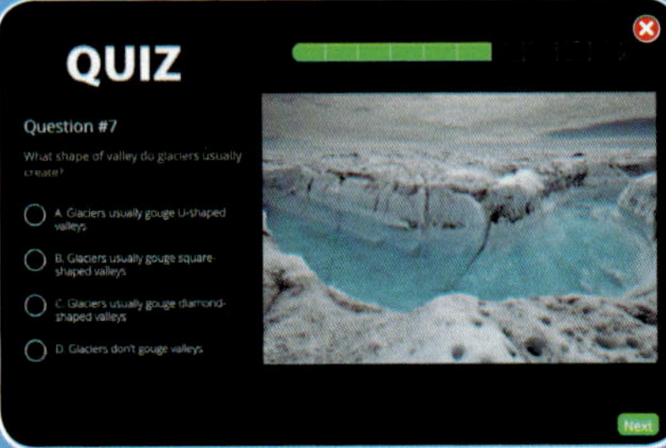

OPTIMIZED FOR

- ✓ TABLETS
- ✓ WHITEBOARDS
- ✓ COMPUTERS
- ✓ AND MUCH MORE!

Published by Smartbook Media Inc.
350 5th Avenue, 59th Floor New York, NY 10118
Website: www.openlightbox.com

Editor: Heather Kissock
Designer: Nick Newton

Library of Congress Cataloging-in-Publication Data
Names: Gagne, Tammy, author.
Title: JPMorgan Chase / Tammy Gagne.
Description: New York, NY : Smartbook Media Inc., [2019] | Series: Corporate America | Includes index.
Identifiers: LCCN 2017048289 (print) | LCCN 2017049834 (ebook) | ISBN 9781510534971 (Multi-User Ebook) | ISBN 9781510534964 (hardcover : alk. paper)
Subjects: LCSH: J.P. Morgan Chase & Co.--Juvenile literature. | Banks and banking--United States--Juvenile literature.
Classification: LCC HG2613.N54 (ebook) | LCC HG2613. N54 J1745 2019 (print) | DDC 332.10973--dc23
LC record available at https://lccn.loc.gov/2017048289

Printed in Brainerd, Minnesota, United States
1 2 3 4 5 6 7 8 9 0 21 20 19 18 17

122017
151217

Photo Credits
Every reasonable effort has been made to trace ownership and to obtain permission to reprint copyright material. The publisher would be pleased to have any errors or omissions brought to its attention so that they may be corrected in subsequent printings. The publisher acknowledges Alamy, Getty Images, iStock, and Shutterstock as its primary image suppliers for this title.